How The

Best
Get
Better®
2

*Excerpt from *The Closing of the Western Mind: The Rise of Faith and the Fall of Reason* by Charles Freeman, © 2003. Knopf. All rights reserved. Used with permission.

Printed in Toronto, Canada. The Strategic Coach Inc., 33 Fraser Avenue, Suite 201, Toronto, Ontario, M6K 3J9. This book was designed and typeset using the Macintosh publishing system by Marilyn Luff. Cover graphic illustrated by Suzanne Noga.

This publication is meant to strengthen your common sense, not to substitute for it. It is also not a substitute for the advice of your doctor, lawyer, accountant, or any of your advisors, personal or professional.

If you would like further information about The Strategic Coach® Program or other Strategic Coach® services and products, please telephone 416.531.7399 or 1.800.387.3206.

Library and Archives Canada Cataloguing in Publication

Sullivan, Dan, 1944-
How the best get better 2 : building an unlimited entrepreneurial future/Dan Sullivan.

ISBN 978-1-897239-11-7

1. Success in business. 2. Entrepreneurship.

I. Title. II. Title: How the best get better two.

HB615.S9432 2007   650.1   C2007-904930-3

This book has a companion set of over two hours of audio recordings that can be downloaded at strategiccoach.com/go/HTBGB2. Either reading the book or listening to the audio will be of benefit. However, the audios contain more stories and examples of the concepts in the book in action. I encourage you to review both in order to receive the greatest impact.

Welcome to

How The Best Get Better® 2

"It takes only one independent and effective rational
mind to change the paradigms of understanding for the
rest of humankind."

Charles Freeman
*The Closing of the Western Mind**

Table of Contents

A Lifetime Of Getting Better

In Book One of *How The Best Get Better*®, we focused on strategies and concepts that would make any entrepreneur in the marketplace more effective. Here in Book Two, we're going to take that a step further to show how entrepreneurs who have the foundation from Book One can take advantage of some extraordinary opportunities that exist in the 21st century.

Book One was based on our observation that the period between the 20th and the 21st centuries was a great entrepreneurial age. Great opportunities opened up for entrepreneurs in many different industries. Much of that had to do with the microchip. Starting in the 1970s and 1980s, the microchip opened the door for millions of entrepreneurs to create independent lives and wonderful lifestyles for themselves around independent businesses.

In Book Two, we're going to look at some extraordinary developments that are taking place in the 21st century. We are now operating in a single global economic system. This is the result of the spread of microtechnology all over the world and also of the collapse of the Soviet Union. Virtually every country in the world is now part of the same economic system. Everyone is trying to create as much entrepreneurial activity in their country as possible. The Internet and advances in shipping have allowed everyone to trade with everyone else. This is no longer just going on at the level of multinational corporations and import-export businesses, but at the level of individual consumers, spurred on by platforms like eBay.

This explosion of entrepreneurial activity makes it a wonderful time to be an entrepreneur if you have your wits about you. Never has there been more opportunity, but with this opportunity has come, in equal measure, a greater amount of complexity and competition. More than ever, it is vital for entrepreneurs to be strategic and focused.

This book and the accompanying audios are designed to show you how you can do your best thinking, and how your best thinking can lead to your best results in this complex global marketplace. We draw on the examples of real entrepreneurs who are operating with great success and personal satisfaction at the forefront of this wave of opportunity. Their

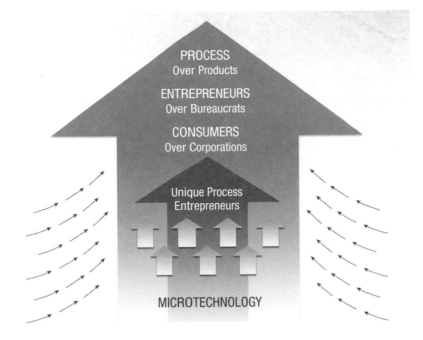

stories are in the audio portion of this presentation, while the book offers a synopsis of the concepts and strategies so you can easily review them.

One thing that is very clear is that the best entrepreneurs always make the world more productive. Millions of entrepreneurs are using their creativity and their ability to create results to move resources from a lower level to a higher level of productivity, which is exactly the definition of entrepreneurship, according to 19th-century economist Jean-Baptiste Say.

The entrepreneurs who will be most rewarded and praised in the 21st century are those whose creativity allows millions of other people to become more productive. To do this, you first need to have a structure that allows you to think creatively about the vast scope of opportunities available to entrepreneurs right now. The six concepts we present here will help to shift the way you look at the world you're operating in. And the six strategies that follow are those we've seen in our work with over 10,000 entrepreneurs to be the most important practical tools to help entrepreneurs achieve extraordinary results in this environment. It is our hope that you will use this material to begin to realize a much bigger and more exciting entrepreneurial future, which will also free you to experience unlimited lifetime growth and an unsurpassed quality of life.

The Commoditization Trap

One of the greatest challenges facing even the most successful entrepreneurs in this early part of the 21st century is that all products and services are quickly becoming commodities. Virtually every product and service can eventually be provided more cheaply by some competitor. Continuous advances in global communication and transportation have made it easier than ever for competitors to copy innovators. Big box stores and corporate consolidation reduce differentiation and favor products and services that can be replicated en masse at low cost.

What this means to entrepreneurs who depend on the sale of these products and services is that the prices they can charge are going down, while the costs of doing business are going up. At some point, it becomes impossible to remain profitable. Entrepreneurs who cannot see their way out of this situation are forced to work longer and harder for less reward, satisfaction, and opportunity. It's such a common dynamic that we've given it a name: The Commoditization Trap.

So close, you can't see it. It's impossible to objectively see the system you're in until you can get a perspective from outside of it. This is why entrepreneurs who deal with the forces of commoditization every day often don't see how The Commoditization Trap works, and as a result get caught up in it. All they know is that things aren't as easy as they used to be, and they don't seem to be getting better. This is demoralizing on a day-to-day basis, and, worse, it keeps them from creating the entrepreneurial lives they want. Trapped by the increasing pressures of competition and complexity, they find themselves unable to realize the very freedoms they hoped to attain when they first decided to become entrepreneurs. Among these are the freedom to control their time, the freedom to earn more money, and the freedom to do what's most meaningful to them.

A permanent escape is necessary. The first step to entrepreneurial success in the 21st century is learning how to escape and permanently avoid The Commoditization Trap. This is what the remaining concepts and strategies in this book will help you to do, and in doing so, you will also open the way to unlimited opportunity for a lifetime of growth and satisfaction from your business.

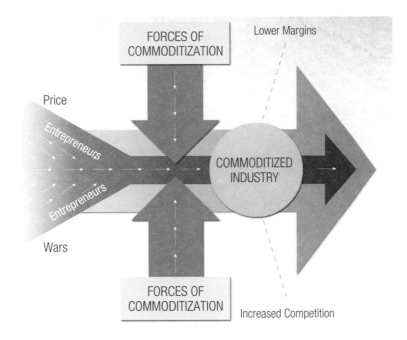

The Experience Monopoly as the remedy. The antithesis of commoditization is to experience constantly increasing customer loyalty and profitability, along with immunity from price comparison and competition. The best entrepreneurs have figured out how to permanently escape The Commoditization Trap by creating a monopoly in the marketplace around an experience that only they can create for their clients.

This is a complete shift from what many entrepreneurs believe is possible for their businesses. It is also what the most successful entrepreneurs with the biggest futures are achieving right now in many different fields. These pioneers have discovered how to bypass what everyone else is doing in the marketplace and create experiences for their clients and customers that are uniquely valued and appreciated. Their clientele begin to see them as crucial to their future success. They realize that what is being provided is something they can't get anywhere else.

Even more important than the experiences themselves is the fact that the entrepreneurs have learned to create them. They have built the structures, processes, and thinking patterns that allow them to create unique value. Even if others try to copy them, they will always be able to out-innovate their competitors because of these capabilities.

The Creative Destruction® LifeCycle

An Austrian economist named Joseph Schumpeter coined the term "creative destruction" in the 1940s to describe the central dynamic of global capitalism. In the capitalist economies of the world, old forms of value creation are continually being destroyed by the creation of new ones. This is how capitalism progresses. This relationship between creation and destruction is the fundamental backdrop for all entrepreneurial activity in the 21st century. To find opportunity and avoid becoming trapped in a world shaped by commoditization, it is essential to be able to see exactly how Creative Destruction® is operating all around us. The Creative Destruction LifeCycle is a model that provides a way to think and talk about this dynamic.

The Creative Zone. Every new turn of the cycle starts with a bypass of something that is old and depleted. When an entrepreneur comes up with a way of doing things that makes the old way obsolete, they are entering the Bypass Stage. Soon, a few savvy others catch on and want to be a part of this new way of doing things because they see how their talents and resources can create even more value by doing so. This is the Emerging Stage, in which there is a lot of uncertainty and excitement. Companies may be disorganized, still getting used to their own success. At some point, word catches on to the point where masses of talent and resources are drawn to this new way of doing things. New structures are built to streamline processes and handle the new growth. This is the Growth Stage in full swing. These three stages—Bypass, Emerging, and Growth—make up the Creative Zone of The Creative Destruction LifeCycle.

The Destruction Zone. At some point, when a growing industry or business model is clearly successful, it begins to attract the attention of those who are more interested in preserving money and status than in creating value for others. Most often, these are lawyers, accountants, and professional executives. Bureaucracy begins to take on a life of its own, and status and hierarchy, policy and efficiency overtake the desire to create value for clientele. People inside and outside the company begin to believe that the company is invincible, that it will always be a leader. This is the onset of the Status Stage. Once a company or industry begins to rest on its laurels, it becomes increasingly difficult for it to innovate in any way that is meaningful to its clientele. A kind of arrogance takes over that cuts it off from being able to respond to its target markets. No longer

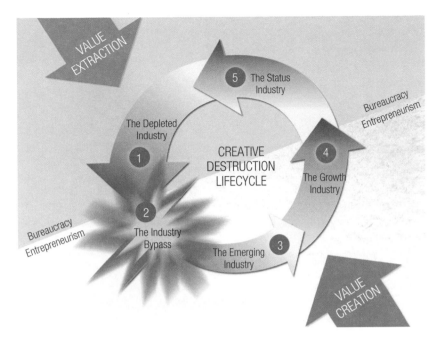

able to draw customers through value creation, it may choose to try to force the market to buy its offerings through legislation or sneaky marketing tactics. It may also decide to offer less for more to increase profits. Consumers who see through this are not impressed and begin to feel cheated. The reputation of the company or industry declines. Talented people in the organization who are committed to value creation and innovation leave to seek better opportunities. Other resources follow suit, flowing toward situations where value is being created, not depleted.

Staying on side. At any given time, there are always ways of doing things, cultures, business models, and industries that are being created at the same time as others are being destroyed. As an entrepreneur, the place to be is in the creative part of the cycle, where all growth and innovation happens. However, the greatest opportunities come about when the destructive part of the cycle frees up resources and opens the way for entrepreneurs to create bypasses for systems and structures that no longer serve people's needs. Thus, both parts of the cycle are needed.

The key to staying in The Creative Zone is always to focus on creating increasing value for your clients and prospects. Any business that retains this focus cannot slip into the Status or Depleted mindset.

Value Creation

Why is it that certain entrepreneurs are better at making themselves unique and indispensable to their clientele? The secret lies in the never-ending creation of new value that others see as crucial.

The remedy to confusion, isolation, and powerlessness. Creating value consists of providing three things: leadership, relationship, and creativity. In a world where endless global change leaves people with a chronic sense of confusion, isolation, and powerlessness, these three things are indispensable. Leadership is providing direction to others in order to help them deal with feelings of confusion that arise out of living in an increasingly complex world. Relationship is providing a new sense of confidence when people feel isolated by change. And creativity is providing new capabilities when people are feeling powerless as a result of change.

Plans, decisions, and actions. Entrepreneurs who continually create new forms of leadership, relationship, and creativity will continue to have increasing opportunity and success. This is because billions of people want new ways to succeed in this changing world and are looking for others to help them do it. In a world shaped by Creative Destruction, people need direction, confidence, and capability to feel good about their futures. They want to know that they are making the right decisions. They want to have plans for the future. They want new methods and tools that will help them take action to deal with changing circumstances and allow them to capture emerging opportunities. They want to know that there are still people and companies they can count on. This kind of help will never be a commodity.

Only those creating value have a future. For entrepreneurs who have nothing to offer but commoditized products and services, the future can look bleak. With nothing to offer but a lower price on an undifferentiated product or service, there is no room to grow and no excitement about the future. However, for entrepreneurs whose aim is always to provide higher quality leadership, relationship, and creativity to their clientele, there is endless opportunity to keep getting better. For these entrepreneurs, the best products and services are only vehicles for providing direction, confidence, and capability. They are conscious that it is not the products that keep their customers coming back, but the value those customers receive that they feel unable to get elsewhere.

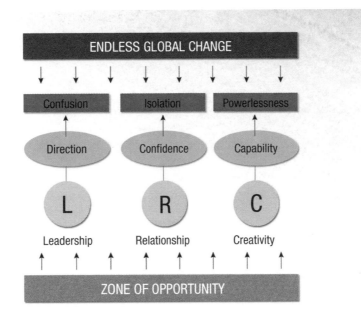

They understand that their own bigger future is tied to creating a bigger future for their clients, customers, and prospects. Creative Destruction works in their favor by ensuring that there will always be new opportunities to create value in new areas.

Value creation brings many rewards. In return for their responsiveness and ability to keep doing things their clients love, these entrepreneurs experience increasing customer loyalty, growing referrals and praise, and the free marketing and PR that come from having a great reputation in the marketplace. Opportunity and resources are attracted to them as people take notice of what they're doing. Great people want to work for and with them. This is entirely the opposite experience to the entrepreneur who is fighting a losing battle in the commoditization game. For that entrepreneur, there are no resources or time left to try to create extra value for clientele. Everything must be reduced and pared down to lower costs. The mentality is one of increasing scarcity rather than increasing abundance.

Entrepreneurs are in a unique position to be able to create value for others. Those who create the most value do it by integrating their unique passions, experience, wisdom, and capabilities into solutions and processes that help others.

The Integrated Entrepreneur™

All innovations occur as a result of someone using their experience in a new way. The greatest inventors and entrepreneurs have been able to come up with new ideas because they saw something, usually something everyone else was seeing, in a different way. They saw different possibilities and different potential—a way to make things better that no one else had ever noticed or been able to act on. An invaluable resource for entrepreneurs is their own unique perspective, which comes from integrating their unique experiences and advantages. The more entrepreneurs can integrate their unique characteristics into what they do, the more success and satisfaction they will experience.

Uniqueness leads to new value creation. Entrepreneurs have an advantage in that they tend to value their own experience more than they value what other people are saying or doing. They are more likely than most people to do something simply because their own experience tells them that it's right, even if no one else has done it that way before. This makes them more innovative in their actions and often more contrarian and comfortable with risk. Because entrepreneurs' growth and success are so directly tied to creating value in the marketplace, their uniqueness is naturally directed toward creating innovations that will benefit others.

There are eight key facets that the best entrepreneurs are always integrating:
1. **Unique experiences.** They are clear about the experiences that have made the biggest difference to them and others around them.
2. **Unique goals.** They are clear about where they want their future progress and achievement to be.
3. **Unique obstacles.** They see all roadblocks as opportunities for growth.
4. **Unique character.** They clearly understand what other people count on them for and where they have a permanent, positive impact.
5. **Unique Ability®.** They understand where their superior skill combines with their passion.
6. **Unique advantages.** They appreciate the assets and situations that give them an advantage.
7. **Unique relationships.** They see where great teamwork is possible with other unique individuals.
8. **Unique value.** They understand the unique difference they make in other people's lives.

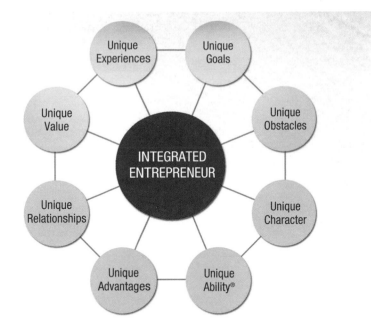

Every entrepreneur has the raw material. The ones who are most successful are those who consciously integrate this self-knowledge into their actions and strategies. They take their own experience—good and bad—and transform it into new concepts and capabilities. Through their businesses, they are constantly able to make the most of all these unique characteristics and, above that, to deepen and strengthen them.

Because they can integrate the facets of their own lives in the face of endless global change, entrepreneurs are in a position to help others do the same. They use their self-created sense of direction to provide others with leadership. They use their self-created sense of confidence to provide others with relationship. And they use their self-created sense of capability to provide others with creativity. When you look at entrepreneurial innovation from this perspective, it's easy to see how there can be even more unique offerings and innovations than there are entrepreneurs. An entrepreneur's ability to integrate turns change that overwhelms others into opportunity and advantages.

The Fundamental Relationship

All business success depends on relationship. You have a relationship with a target market of people or organizations to whom you deliver value. In return, they reward you with money, referrals, future business, and a growing reputation, among other things. The best entrepreneurs understand how to leverage this circular relationship with the outside world so that it becomes not only a powerful money-making system, but an engine for continually increasing their growth and satisfaction. It is through making the most of this Fundamental Relationship that they are able to escape commoditization and also have the world fund the development of their greatest abilities and the achievement of their biggest goals.

You may remember that I talked about "delegating everything except genius" in the original *How The Best Get Better*®. At this next level of success, entrepreneurs not only focus on the superior skills they have a passion for, which we call Unique Ability, they use their Unique Ability to create value for a very specific target group of people who appreciate it the most. Rather than trying to be all things to all people, they have found the clients and customers who receive the most value from what they have to offer and who demonstrate this by writing cheques. They create strong relationships with these people, taking the time to learn what they most fear losing, what they're most excited about gaining, and what strengths they already have that they would like to see leveraged. By doing this, they become a key contributor to their bigger futures. This knowledge allows these entrepreneurs to find ways to use their Unique Ability to provide even more direction, confidence, and capability to more people just like their best clients and customers. As they do this, their rewards continue to grow, so everything in the system keeps increasing within The Fundamental Relationship.

A structure for lifetime growth. The Fundamental Relationship is really, then, just a simple way to focus in on the process of continuous growth through value creation using your Unique Ability. Eventually, what evolves out of this growth and the learning that happens along the way is a Unique Process™ for value creation. Its uniqueness is guaranteed by the uniqueness of your wisdom and experience, your relationships with your clients and customers, and your knowledge of how to create value for them.

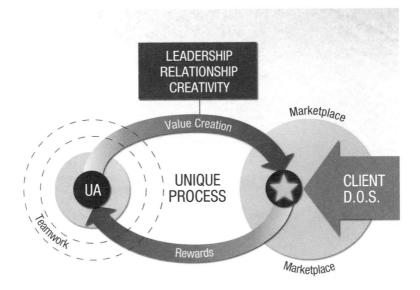

Sometimes imitated, never equaled. When a process evolves in this organic way, based on constant feedback and refinement, it embodies so much wisdom that it becomes impossible to imitate. While it seems simple and natural to the team that develops it over time, there are so many subtle systems and processes behind the scenes supporting the quality of the unique experience that, often, competitors can't even really understand *what* is being done, much less how it is being accomplished. They may try to say they're doing what you're doing, but anyone who experiences what you have to offer will quickly see that though they may have the words, they don't have the tune.

It is by continually strengthening The Fundamental Relationship that entrepreneurs can permanently avoid The Commoditization Trap and keep growing, prospering, and increasing their freedom and resources to create exactly the life they want.

In the Strategies that follow, we will talk about how to leverage your Fundamental Relationship to maximize your freedom and growth. However, first, we have one more concept to cover that goes to the heart of how the best entrepreneurs see themselves and how that frees them to create extraordinary value and prosperity.

The Double Shift

Many entrepreneurs, even successful ones, do not see themselves first and foremost as entrepreneurs. Rather, they see themselves as belonging to some industry or profession, or as the owner of a particular type of company that is tied to the provision of a certain group of products or services. In doing this, they, mostly unconsciously, tie themselves to the world of commodities and to the limitations of established, undifferentiated ways of doing things within their industry. To escape from a dependence on commodities, and from being turned into commodities themselves, a shift to a new concept of their own identity is needed.

This shift usually happens in two stages:

Stage 1: I am an entrepreneur with a specialty in *x*. The first stage happens when an entrepreneur sees themselves as an entrepreneur first and foremost, with a specialty in whatever industry or profession they have experience in. For instance, rather than being a lawyer, they would think of themselves as an entrepreneur with a specialty in law. This change in perspective frees them up to think like an entrepreneur. As mentioned in the introduction, the 19th-century French economist, Jean-Baptiste Say, defined an entrepreneur as someone who takes resources from a lower level to a higher level of productivity. Within the scope of that definition, there are myriad opportunities for any entrepreneur with any specialty. While their competitors are increasingly caught in The Commoditization Trap, entrepreneurs who make this shift experience an instant increase in their responsiveness, creativity, and adaptability.

Increasing productivity is about creating more value using the same resources and finding easier, faster, better, and cheaper ways of getting things done. Experienced entrepreneurs have a lot of accumulated wisdom about how things work in their area of specialty, but they need a perspective from beyond their industry to be able to see how to use that knowledge in new ways to create new and better solutions. Often, these better solutions come in the form of shortcuts you can offer your clientele to help them get results in an easier, faster, and ultimately less costly way. These shortcuts have a value of their own and can be sold separately, in addition to the commodities that may be required for their implementation.

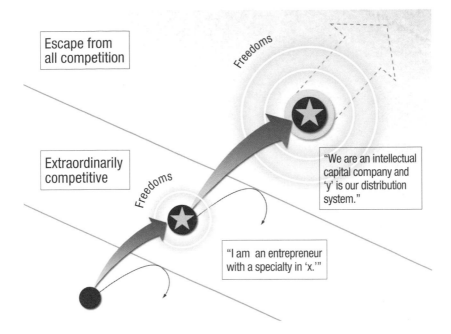

Escape from all competition

Freedoms

Extraordinarily competitive

Freedoms

"We are an intellectual capital company and 'y' is our distribution system."

"I am an entrepreneur with a specialty in 'x.'"

Stage 2: We are an intellectual capital company and *y* is our distribution system. The second shift takes the entrepreneur and their company to an entirely new level. When you continually create innovative forms of value, others in your industry tend to notice. Often, when they realize they can't replicate what you're doing, they want to buy your process—your intellectual capital. At some point, it makes more sense for you to profit from the licensing, teaching, or sale of your intellectual capital than merely from its direct delivery to the end client. When you begin to sell the process itself, you become an intellectual capital company, and that process becomes simply a distribution system. This is tremendously liberating because once you've created one piece of valuable intellectual capital, you are able to create others the same way—by focusing on the evolving needs of your clients and drawing from your accumulated wisdom. By innovating at this level, you stay well ahead of the forces of commoditization and instead become a leader in a new industry of your own making.

As an intellectual capital company, you are no longer operating within the confines of any industry. In fact, you are likely to transform the industries you do business with because your innovative methods will impact what other companies do and what consumers come to expect in that area.

The D.O.S. Conversation®

The very best entrepreneurs in the 21st century do not sell products or services; what they really sell are transformative conversations. In other words, they've created a conversation in the marketplace in which people can transform the crucial issues they're facing and come up with breakthroughs. The conversation most people want to have is about their future growth, progress, and success. This is a conversation you can have with anyone. And this future is not just about their business life, it's about their personal life as well.

The biggest problem people have today is complexity. It doesn't matter who you are or what you do, there's just far too much complexity in all of our lives. People have so much on their minds that it's difficult for them to even identify what their problems really are. At Strategic Coach®, we like to say that the problem is never the problem; the problem is that people don't even know how to think about the problem. The D.O.S. Conversation® is a way to create immediate value for people by giving them an opportunity to think about their problems in a clear and constructive way. It's also the first step to all future value creation.

D.O.S.® stands for dangers, opportunities, and strengths. The D.O.S. Conversation starts with The R-Factor Question®, which you may remember from Book One: "If we were meeting here three years from today, what has to have happened during that three-year period for you to be happy about your progress?"

Once you've established where the person wants to be in the future using The R-Factor Question, the next step is to find out what dangers they would most like to eliminate, what opportunities they would most like to capture and maximize, and what strengths they would like to leverage to reach that future. This allows you to tap in to what drives them emotionally. Dangers are connected to fear, a powerfully motivating emotion. Opportunities are connected to excitement, also a key motivator. Strengths are the foundation of their sense of confidence, but when people are preoccupied with their dangers, they often lose sight of what's working in their favor.

It's all about them. The best thing about this conversation is that it lays the groundwork for a successful future business relationship *without ever*

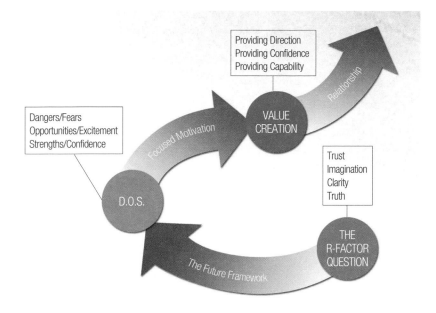

talking about products or services. After having been asked these questions, people feel listened to and understood. A level of trust and understanding is created that they don't get in other business settings. A soon as you have this conversation, you completely differentiate yourself from any seller of commodities the person has ever encountered. You wouldn't ask these questions if you weren't really concerned with creating value for them. The entire conversation is about them. All the leadership, relationship, and creativity you can provide for them will have to relate to their D.O.S. issues to register with them as value creation. After all, they are the ones who will judge whether you have truly provided them with direction, confidence, and capability.

As long as you keep using your clients' and customers' evolving D.O.S. as the foundation for your innovations, you will automatically be immune to commoditization and to slipping into The Destruction Zone of the Creative Destruction LifeCycle.

The D.O.S. Conversation is the foundation for all the value you will create in the marketplace. But it's only half the picture. The other half comes from your unique wisdom and how you use it to address your clientele's D.O.S. issues. This brings us to the next strategy, The Experience Transformer®.

The Experience Transformer®

Perhaps the reason so many entrepreneurs still focus their conversations on products and services rather than on their clientele's D.O.S. is that they wouldn't know what to do with the D.O.S. information even if they had it. The best entrepreneurs take this information and use it as raw material for a transformation. They transform existing experience into breakthroughs. The reason they are able to do this for others is that they've practiced by doing it with their own experiences, both positive and negative. This is how wisdom is accumulated and how all great entrepreneurs keep getting better, no matter what life throws at them.

The Experience Transformer process has four main parts:

1. All progress starts by telling the truth. The first step is simple: Always be very honest about the experience you've had. One of the biggest obstacles that keeps people from solving their problems is that they don't describe what's really happening. They do this to try to avoid some of the pain of the experience, but, actually, that pain can be very useful fuel to help bring about the change that's necessary for a breakthrough. So begin by acknowledging what really happened.

2. What worked? The next step is to focus on what worked in the situation. This can be difficult if you've experienced a setback or a frustration, because it looks like everything is bad. But even in the worst situations, if you look, you'll often find that there were lots of things that did work.

3. What didn't work? Next, look at what didn't work. If the situation is negative, this is usually easy. If it's positive, this may be the trickier of the two.

4. If we could do it again, how would we do it differently? Pretend you're a film director and you're going to roll back the tape and decide how to do it over. You have the opportunity to learn from what worked and what didn't, and to make different decisions for the future. What will you change, knowing what you now know?

Once this way of extracting wisdom from experience becomes natural, it also becomes something you can do for others. The best entrepreneurs are constantly helping others to transform their experiences.

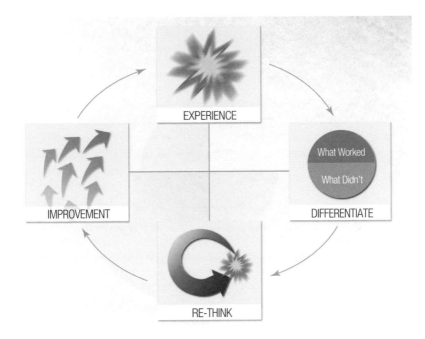

EXPERIENCE

What Worked

What Didn't

DIFFERENTIATE

RE-THINK

IMPROVEMENT

These may be experiences that are similar to ones the entrepreneur has had, or they may be experiences that they have seen many of their clients go through. Either way, they have wisdom that can be applied to help create better outcomes in the future.

Since Creative Destruction is always causing new negative situations in the world, there will continue to be an endless number of experiences for entrepreneurs to transform. The more people feel confused, isolated, and powerless, the more opportunities there will be to improve their situations by providing leadership, relationship, and creativity. The D.O.S. Conversation clearly lays out what needs to be transformed, along with the desired outcome of the transformation.

As entrepreneurs become very skilled at transforming similar experiences that come from people with similar D.O.S. issues, they may find that they develop a Unique Process that can benefit many people. This brings us to our next strategy: Packaging Your Unique Process.

Packaging Your Unique Process™

An intellectual capital company requires a different kind of business model than a provider of commodities. The Unique Process is the basis of this model. Every experienced entrepreneur has a Unique Process, but, being focused on products and services, most never recognize it, and still fewer charge for it. Most entrepreneurs actually give away what their clients value most as a loss leader to sell more products and services.

To realize the potential for freedom and growth that being an entrepreneur in a world governed by Creative Destruction offers, it is necessary to not only charge for the real value you create, but to recognize it as the central core of your business. *The Unique Process is the ideal business structure for the 21st-century entrepreneur.*

Unique Processes™ evolve when entrepreneurs take the D.O.S. of their clients and prospects, and use their wisdom to turn this information into breakthroughs. After many repetitions and refinements, it becomes clear that you have a process that consistently works to address a certain set of D.O.S. issues. Packaging the process simply means identifying each step where value is created and plainly and clearly communicating these steps to the client or customer in advance, so they can see how you're going to help them achieve the solution they're looking for.

Selling direction, confidence, and capability. Selling a Unique Process is really selling clientele a new game plan to help them get to the future they want, with clearly defined deliverables along the way. When people see the solution to their problems laid out like this, they understand what their commitment needs to be, as well as what you're going to do to get them to the result they want. This gives them a tremendous amount of confidence. It makes them feel like you're a partner in creating their bigger future. They are free from confusion, isolation, and powerlessness in this area of their lives.

Free from dependency on commodity sales. Although the implementation of the process may require products and services that clientele could obtain elsewhere, perhaps even at a lower price, they are much more likely to keep all their business with you because you understand them and where they want to go. Even if they do choose to go to

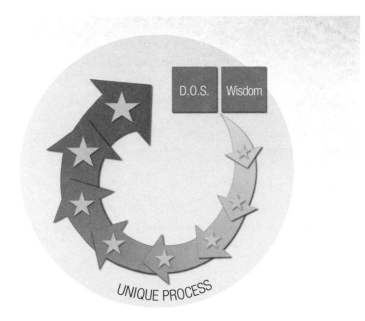

someone else for some of these commodities, it doesn't matter to you because you're getting paid for the process independently, and this is where the relationship and the loyalty are.

Constant improvement is built in. Every time you deliver your Unique Process, you deepen your mastery of the D.O.S. issues it addresses. Every new client situation adds to your wisdom and expertise at delivering value in this area. By constantly refining the process to incorporate more of this evolving wisdom, you continually differentiate yourself from all competitors. In the process, you develop valuable intellectual capital that can itself be sold.

Freedom is the ultimate reward. As you strengthen your Fundamental Relationship, your value creation and rewards constantly increase. And being independent of commodities and the outside pressures of conforming to a role within an industry, you can also increase your freedom in the four areas of time, money, relationship, and purpose. You are increasingly able to free yourself from external circumstances that determine how you spend your time, how much money you can make, who you work with, and how useful you can be. This makes the Unique Process the ideal structure for any entrepreneur who wants to keep getting better throughout their lifetime.

The Five Circles

Most entrepreneurs associate growth with selling more products and services, but anyone who understands commoditization knows that there isn't much leverage or freedom in this as a long-term growth strategy. At best, entrepreneurs who pursue this strategy will be constantly battling the forces of commoditization, seeing their marketing costs rise, while their margins shrink and their quality of life decreases. The Unique Process approach demands a different kind of growth strategy, one that enables entrepreneurs to develop over a lifetime in a completely unique fashion. This strategy can be envisioned by looking at a model called The Five Circles.

Circles 1 to 3: From product to process. The circles show the phases that a Unique Process-based business goes through as it evolves. All entrepreneurs start by selling a product. Eventually, they run into a problem in that all their competitors are selling the same product. The solution is to wrap the product in a service that can be customized to the buyer. This differentiates them from competitors, but eventually a new problem arises that gets in the way of growth: The product is still a commodity whose price is determined by the market, and the entrepreneur isn't receiving any payment for the value-added service. This is where the packaged Unique Process comes in. Each stage of the transformative game plan is named, and more stages are added to create additional value that the customer pays for separately from the commodities involved in executing the game plan. Now the entrepreneur is getting paid for the value-added services as well as the product.

Circles 4 and 5: Unique community and culture. Eventually, the Unique Process, because of its originality and naming conventions, gives rise to a new way of talking about the problem and its solutions—a unique language. This unique language binds together those who have participated in the Unique Process and creates a unique community. The influence of a powerful, loyal community eventually creates a unique culture of people who feel connected to and supportive of the process and its attributes.

This is happening every day, all around us. Think about it: Who ever heard the term "podcast" before millions of people started using iPods? Now millions of people, even those without actual iPods, are using this

language and are connected, with varying degrees of participation, to the community and the culture that Apple initiated and continues to nurture. Many people can tell from a distance if someone has a genuine Apple product or another brand. This may tell them something about the person, such as whether they are a Mac user, which has its own set of cultural associations. These ideas and the language around them have become embedded as cultural references, and they started with a company that created a product that went through the evolution of The Five Circles.

This growth path is available only to entrepreneurial companies that have a D.O.S.-based Unique Process. What it does is allow the company to create an "experience monopoly" around a set of transformative experiences that clients and customers see as crucial to their greater enjoyment and satisfaction. Though others may try to copy parts of this experience, the unique community and culture guarantee that they will always be seen as imitators. Loyal members of the community will continue to defend the original experience and communicate its advantages to others. As the entrepreneur who is the creator of this Unique Process, you have the experience that the world is on your side—a complete contrast to the entrepreneur who is still trying to grow merely by selling more commoditized products and services.

The Front Stage/Back Stage Model®

Providing a unique experience is about more than packaging. It's about being able to consistently deliver on what you promise. In this respect, all business is like a theater with a front stage and a backstage. For clients to have a great experience of the front stage, many more things have to be working backstage, behind the scenes. All business success and failure is determined by the integrated quality of your Front Stage and your Back Stage.

Front Stage encompasses everything that your clientele experiences about your business. Great Front Stage experiences require great Back Stage skills, methods, and teamwork. Building a successful entrepreneurial company, then, requires that you focus on developing both your Front Stage and Back Stage.

If you think about the times when you experience a great Front Stage, you'll see that they have three basic components: First, the experience is uniquely positive—you want to tell other people about it; second, the packaging is impressive and differentiated from all other experiences; and, third, you receive unique value in the form of direction, confidence, and capability.

Great Back Stage is the foundation. Here's what is usually happening Back Stage in order to consistently create those great experiences: First, all the Front Stage experiences are supported with great systems and capabilities; second, great teamwork takes place among people who are using their Unique Ability; and, third, great communication and coordination takes place among all the individuals and teams who are part of creating the experience.

Good Front Stage is always rewarded, and bad Front Stage is always punished. People base their decisions to buy and refer on the quality of their experiences. As an entrepreneur, it can be tempting to look only at the Front Stage because most entrepreneurs have great Front Stage skills in the area of sales or customer relationships. However, without that strong Back Stage, your Front Stage will only be able to grow so much before it begins to falter.

An exceptional Back Stage may be invisible to most clients and customers,

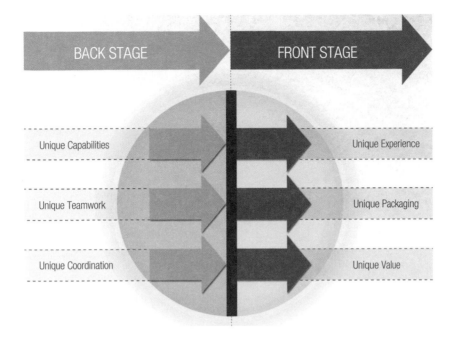

Unique Capabilities

Unique Teamwork

Unique Coordination

Unique Experience

Unique Packaging

Unique Value

and it should be, because it's not what they want to see. They are there for what's on the Front Stage. But where it really shows up is in your ability to consistently meet or exceed their highest expectations. This is what people tell their friends about. It's what they feel good about being part of. It's what they look forward to more of in the future. We all love feeling special. It stands out from the many times we get treated like everyone else, or worse, like we're not even a person but just another transaction.

Following through with integrity. When you start a business relationship with The D.O.S. Conversation, it sets high expectations. You have just treated your prospect or client as a person with their own fears, hopes, and strengths. You have listened to them in a way they may never have been listened to before in a business setting. A strong Front Stage and Back Stage working together is the way to ensure that the respect and value you've demonstrated for their individuality and humanity get carried through into every aspect of your interaction. This is what builds a fiercely loyal, devoted, long-term clientele. For any business to grow through the stages of The Five Circles to the point where it spawns a unique community and culture, it needs to have a great Front Stage and a great Back Stage to support it.

The Three Sales

Most entrepreneurs are very good at selling. They feel highly focused and passionate while doing it. They are at their most imaginative and charming. They are great listeners, capable of really getting inside the other person's head and empathizing with them. It brings out all their best qualities and is the key to their success and confidence. Talk to any group of entrepreneurs about selling, and their eyes light up and they immediately get more excited. Then talk about those times when they're not selling, when they have to be Back Stage, and all that energy goes away.

The reason for this is that most entrepreneurs view what they do on the Front Stage as radically different from what they do when they go Back Stage. On the Front Stage, they get to sell, but on the Back Stage, they feel they have to "manage." This seems to take a whole different set of skills and inclinations, usually ones that don't seem to come as naturally or to generate such confidence.

This final strategy helps entrepreneurs take their selling skills and use them on the Back Stage as well as the Front Stage to create the kind of results they want in every part of their business. It's called The Three Sales, and here's why:

The very best entrepreneurs are masters of three different kinds of sales. There is the "money sale," which happens Front Stage. This is the kind of selling we're all familiar with. But there are also two other kinds of sales that happen Back Stage. These are "freedom sales" and "capability sales." Before I get into what these sales are about, let's look at what selling really is. Selling has two parts: First, it involves engaging other people intellectually with a desirable future result, and then it requires enabling them to emotionally commit to the achievement of that result.

The money sale is a sale you make on the Front Stage by inspiring others to part with their money in return for value you create for them.

The freedom sale is a sale you make Back Stage by inspiring others to free up your time so you can focus on making more money sales.

The capability sale is a sale you make Back Stage by inspiring others to bring new capabilities to your entrepreneurial company.

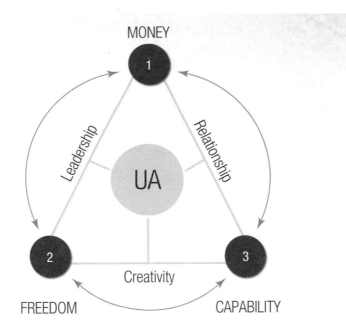

All three of these types of sales require exactly the same skills and the same basic approach. This means if you're good at making money sales, you'll be good at the other two kinds of sales as well. If you're finding that you can't get people to free up your time the way you'd like them to, consider whether you've really tried to sell them on the idea. The same goes for getting people to contribute their best capabilities and energies. Approach the situation as you would any Front Stage sale, and you're likely to get a much more positive response.

Each type of sale reinforces the other two. The more freedom sales and capability sales you make, the easier it is to make money sales. More money sales give you more resources to make freedom sales and capability sales, and so on. Focusing on just these three kinds of sales greatly simplifies an entrepreneur's daily activities while dramatically improving results on both the Front and Back Stage. By just doing what they do best—selling—entrepreneurs can continually improve their businesses and create value for both their clients and their team members. Nothing more is needed than to look for the next sales opportunity that will have the biggest positive impact.

A Road Map To Freedom

How The Best Get Better® 2 calls for entrepreneurs to take the next steps toward creating the kind of business that provides a platform for lifetime growth and a unique quality of life. The concepts and strategies you have just read, and perhaps listened to, provide a road map to transform your experience of being an entrepreneur into one where you have unprecedented freedom and opportunity. To do so is to realize the full potential that the entrepreneurial life has to offer at a time in history when it has never offered more.

Many entrepreneurs are already doing this. In the audios, we have tried to provide a wide cross-section of stories about entrepreneurs who are living these transformed lives, so you can see what they have achieved and also how varied their experiences are. These entrepreneurs are all Strategic Coach® Program participants whom we know well and see on a regular basis. There are many more examples we could have drawn on if we'd had unlimited space. In fact, we see more and more entrepreneurs embark on this path every day. They come from almost every industry and from all over the globe. What they have in common is a desire to have a higher level experience of what it means to be an entrepreneur. They want their entrepreneurial lives to support the achievement of all their life's goals and to do this in a way that is aligned with their values and passions.

Unique Process is the key. The Unique Process, which integrates Unique Ability and The D.O.S. Conversation, provides the backbone for this transformation. It allows entrepreneurs to escape from the scarcity mentality of an economy governed by commoditization and competition to the realm of Unique Experience, where it is possible to have a monopoly on a way of creating unique value for your clientele. Ultimately, this is a much more satisfying place to be.

Role models and transformers. Unique Process entrepreneurs are already shaping up to be among the most important role models in the 21st century. They are significant agents of change who are revered as examples of what individual creativity and initiative can accomplish. Entrepreneurs like this are a good part of the reason why many young people today want to be entrepreneurs, whereas 30 years ago, their forebears at the same age wanted to work for large institutions or corporations.

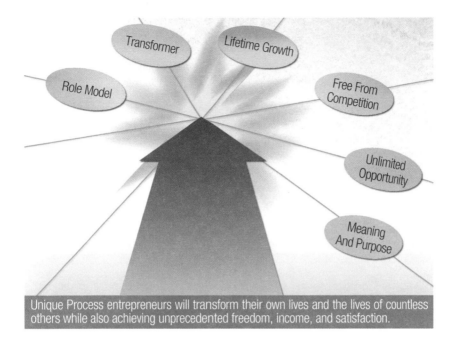

Unique Process entrepreneurs will transform their own lives and the lives of countless others while also achieving unprecedented freedom, income, and satisfaction.

At the same time, Unique Process entrepreneurs are transforming a number of industries by creating bypasses that make old ways of doing things obsolete. In the next century, we will see entrepreneurs come to be recognized as the prime drivers of positive change in many areas that go beyond the traditional realm of business. Their reach will be limited only by what they are passionate about changing because their skills at value creation apply across all areas of life.

This map is good for a century of change. Creative Destruction will keep on providing more and more opportunities as it increases peoples' feelings of confusion, isolation, and powerlessness. All of this will continue to generate endless opportunities for entrepreneurs to find ways to provide leadership, relationship, and creativity as the remedy. What this means is that entrepreneurs who follow the map provided by *How The Best Get Better*®, Books One and Two, will find that this approach is good for a lifetime. The principles will always apply. They will continue to lead to freedom from the forces that increasingly constrain others, and also the freedom to experience a uniquely satisfying, meaningful, rewarding, and fulfilling life.

Where The Best Get Better

Understanding the concepts and strategies in this book is the initial step toward a more rich and fulfilling entrepreneurial life. To make this life a reality, however, much more is required. In our experience, three key elements greatly facilitate this process:

1. **A commitment** on the part of the entrepreneur to a program of activity over a period of years to achieve measurable improvements in all areas of their work and personal life.
2. **A structure of accountability** that keeps the entrepreneur focused on these goals and improvements.
3. **Entrepreneurial concepts and strategies** that enable the goals and improvements to be translated into daily actions.

The Strategic Coach Program. All the concepts and strategies of *How The Best Get Better® 2* come from The Strategic Coach Program, a lifetime focusing structure and process for highly successful entrepreneurs. Before joining us, participants in the Program were already successful as entrepreneurs in a wide variety of industries. However, most had found that, despite their success, they encountered a Ceiling of Complexity™ that blocked their further growth and development.

As a result of this ceiling, many found that they had enormous opportunities, but couldn't get to them. Others felt there was so much opportunity that it was overwhelming. They spent too much time on non-productive activities, and experienced tension between their business and personal lives. They often felt out of control and off track. Entrepreneurial life was not taking them where they wanted to go, or at least not quickly enough. In extreme cases, their health and relationships suffered, and the rewards of being an entrepreneur were overshadowed by the costs.

To add to their frustrations, many discovered that their businesses were being increasingly *commoditized*—that is, they were forced to compete on price in a field crowded with competitors coming at them from all directions. This increased their costs, decreased their profits, and added new levels of complexity and longer hours to their daily work life.

In short, all of these entrepreneurs were ready for a fundamental

change—a breakthrough in the way they approached their businesses and their lives. **They were ready for The Strategic Coach Program.**

The Strategic Coach Program is organized on a workshop basis, offering a full-day session every 90 days at two levels, The Strategic Coach® Signature Program and The 10x Ambition Program™. Only experienced and successful entrepreneurs are eligible: *A net income equal to or greater than US/CA$100,000 (or UK£100,000)—earned over the previous 12-month period—is an entry requirement.*

Four fundamental benefits. Each individual comes to Strategic Coach for unique reasons and pursues a unique plan of progress. However, after the first three years, participants derive the following four benefits:

- **Everyone eliminates all the "stuff" and messes** that interfere with concentration and productivity.
- **Everyone experiences greatly increased focus** on their most important activities, relationships, and opportunities.
- **Everyone experiences a dramatically increased quality of life**—based on a higher quantity and quality of free time.
- **Everyone develops confidence in their Unique Ability**—and in the Unique Ability® Teamwork that systematically transforms this Unique Ability into genius and the foundation for a Unique Process-based business.

The successful entrepreneurs who join The Strategic Coach Program usually decide they need a change about a year before they find out about the Program. They decide that things must change; they just need a structure to help that happen.

If The Strategic Coach Program is the structure you've been looking for, please call 416.531.7399 or 1.800.387.3206. If you would like further information about other Strategic Coach® services and products, please call us at the above numbers or visit our website at *strategiccoach.com.*